The 7 Spells of the New Conference People 2.0

The 7 Spells of the New Conference People 2.0

Dan Ake

Dedication

This book is dedicated to the two people that most influenced my development as a conference leader and expert. They will recognize themselves after reading this dedication. The fruits of the labor put into this book are reflected in all the programs that my team and I have structured and deployed toward organizing many successful conferences, conventions, and trade shows.

All my thanks to the Successful Conference team that every day helps conference executives, sales, marketing, or operations professionals transform themselves from being traditional conference persons into new "Conference People 2.0," able to make their conferences the most successful ones they could have ever imagined.

Table of Contents

*"It is not the strongest of the species that survives
nor the most intelligent that survives.
It is the one that is the most adaptable to change."*

-    Charles Darwin -

Introduction

How to Use this Book of Spells

Who is This Book For?

This book is designed to help all those involved in organizing conferences, and who I will refer to in my book as "conference people". They include:
- conference executives
- conference producers
- conference marketing staff
- conference sales staff
- conference managers
- conference operations staff

As well as
- convention center staff
- venue staff in charge of conferences

This book has been structured to elucidate the profound changes in the conference and trade show industry and to help conference people acquire the skills not only to survive, but also to propel their career to the next level. The industry is facing profound changes—a fact that we must accept.

To meet the challenges of this "evolving" industry means employing new ways of doing our job and using the powerful new weapons that are becoming increasingly available for each of us to make our next conference the most successful one we have ever imagined.

A new era has arrived. The conference people that figure out how to harness the power of new rules to their full advantage will dance on the graves of those who don't and will lead their market.

How to be part of these "Conference People 2.0" is what this book is all about.

If you are in charge of a convention center, a special entry in this Book of Spells has been written to help you meet the needs of your customers. It is recommended that you start with your add-on in Appendix 1.

If you are in charge of a venue, a special entry in this Book of Spells has been detailed for you. It is recommended that you start with your add-on in Appendix 2.

The Magic Words

Each chapter ends with a magic word that will open your eyes to the tremendous set of opportunities around you.

అ◆ఒ

Chapter 1
Magic for Conference People

The Pledge

The first part of a magic trick is called "The Pledge." That is to say, the setup. A magician turns to his audience and introduces "something that is familiar to you" and announces that he will turn it into something extraordinary.

That's exactly what I'm going to do here.

I'm going to take something that you know: "You, as a conference person." Yes, I am going to take you. And I'm going to turn you into something extraordinary: meaning someone capable of successfully using the "7 Spells of the new Conference People 2.0."

Just imagine having the power these 7 Spells offer when you want, when you need them, on demand.
Before the end of this book or video, you will know how these spells work.

And more than that, you will have a protective shield for your career in the conference and trade show industry.

Whoa!

The Spells

But what are these spells?
Imagine when you will be able to master these:

Spell #1: Reveal the hottest topics for my industry

Spell #2: Attract the most outstanding speakers

Spell #3: Enable my next conference to be sold out

Spell #4: Add significant revenues to my next conference

Spell #5: Make my president happy

Spell #6: Make my next conference the most successful and memorable one for my participants

Spell # 7: Give me the power to stay on top and turn the stress away on demand

These are what I pledge to offer you in this book.

The Turn

The second part of a magic trick is where the magician makes something ordinary do something extraordinary. At that time, if you're looking for the secret to this...you won't find it.

I wish I could resist telling you the secret and bring you to the supplication stage, with you begging me to learn how to do the turn yourself.

I myself am a fan of magic, and so is my daughter. We used to play magic games together, experience new ideas, and compete with each other. And I have always told her to keep the first commandment of a magician: "Never tell the secret to anybody! Not even to your mom."

Even though I am not a pure magician, I have had such pleasure teaching my daughter how to do magic. Seeing her doing things she thought she couldn't do and which others qualify as extraordinary is a real joy for me.

When she fills the room with wonder and fascinates her friends with magic tricks, I am a loving father in a state of ecstasy.

The Apprenticeship

In every apprenticeship, apprentices start with easy exercises that they can immediately perform with no great effort with ingredients they have around them. Little practice is involved to do the job. And then as they become more confident, they invest in deeper learning and more sophisticated tools so they can build bigger turns with more impressive results.

The intent of this book is not to transform you into a master, whereby you can use these 7 Spells at their full power. The goals of this book are to:

- show you how you can get results with a very simple use of these spells
- direct you to the path to develop yours skills for each of them, and
- give you the will to perform the following steps to master all of these 7 Spells that will definitely change your life and career

Each chapter contains:

- the principles and distinctive characteristics of a spell
- step-by-step training to get your first immediate results
- the process and the results you will get using the spell at its full strength. If this chapter addresses your current concerns, it will bring new light to them.

The Prestige

This is the third act of magic called, "The Prestige." This is the part with the twists and turns, where lives hang in the balance, and you see something shocking you've never seen before. And I am going to experience this with you before the end of this book.

When you amaze your peers by mastering these "7 Spells of the new Conference People 2.0," you have to realize that somebody, Dan Ake, is experiencing ecstasy, thanks to you.

When others are impressed by the results of your new skills, you will give me the greatest gratification.

That's the reason why I'm not going to assume the pose of a real magician and keep the secrets to myself. I'm going to share them with you. My gift to you is that you will understand how these spells work before the end of this book.

Chapter 2
Where the Magic is

Your Audience

So, as a magician does with his apprentices, I am going to first speak about the audience (the people who are around you). Then I will show you how to handle what comes from them, which could be an attitude full of negative vibes. Many of us are impacted by the despondency prevalent within our industry. I say "many of us," because your magician is a conference person too and remains unaffected by it. Just to tell you a few words about where Dan Ake comes from and how he became the one who received this ability to transmit these powerful skills to you...

Your Magician

Since the beginning, there has been something in him fixated on searching out how to make things better, easier, and more effective. That's the reason why ten years ago the press used to qualify him as an "artificial intelligence expert." His first job, indeed, was to create algorithms that were written to make Internet websites more intelligent, first in the Internet banking area, then in the social networks area.

Thereafter, he discovered the conference and trade show industry and became a conference person. At this time, he experienced a breakthrough: he discovered that the Internet and conferences have something major in common. They both help people meet each other. They both help people meet the right person.

For the past six years, he has been working on developing practical uses of the Internet and social media for conferences and trade shows. He is the founder of the "Successful Conference Academy," wherein his team structured all their research results into easy to understand, practical, comprehensive educational material, enabling any conference person to easily integrate it into structuring events.

He is also the creator of the "Conference People 2.0" masterminds.

The name "Conference People 2.0" comes from Internet history. When the Internet passed through a terrible crisis called the Internet bubble in 2000–2001, it was forced to reinvent itself in order to survive.

The new version of the Internet was referred to as Internet 2.0, and has come to mean an internet that is more powerful, stronger, and more capable to withstand upcoming crises.

And that's exactly what "Conference People 2.0" means: conference people who have new skills, who are *you* more powerful, stronger, and more capable of withstanding upcoming crises.

In order to always stay on the cutting edge of what's new and efficient in regard to both conference practices and Internet and social media novelties, Dan Ake joined "Market Leaders Factory," a company whose mission is to bring products or services being top ranked on Google, worldwide or locally.

The author also has set up a consulting company, Successful Conference, which he co-founded to share this practical knowledge adapted to our industry with his clients.

As soon as this efficient framework appeared in the convention market, people started to ask Mr. Ake to provide them with a tool, a guide to follow in implementing the practical strategies he offered in their day-to-day lives and jobs. That's the reason why, apart from the complete training programs and "done-for-you" systems delivered by the Successful Conference team, he decided to write this book.

Regarding the transformational effect on the people discovering these concepts, he has written it like a novel about magic.

Why We Need Magic

Let's talk about the bad messengers, those who speak about the travel crisis, the bad economy, cost reductions, and volcanoes that have had an impact on convention balance sheets. They're up in arms about the avian flu having been responsible for a temporary downturn in convention industry profits and much more, including online conferencing systems that are supposed to take the place of conventions and trade shows.

Let's soak it, for the very last time. Once you know how to use the 7 Spells of the new "Conference People 2.0," you will understand that all of this is "B.S."

We conducted a survey among convention and trade show people in order to have a precise view of what they think about social media. We asked if they use the tools it offers, how they use them, and if they were satisfied by the results.

The data we gathered is impressive. Their analysis can be summarized into three words: anxiety, doubt, and fear.

Here are some of the common quotes we received:

Doubts about the future of the industry:
- "The main issue in regard to business conferences is the lack of tangible value."
- "The standard format of our conferences is too far from the actual structure that allows people to learn and engage."
- "Most of conferences failed to deliver something that people see valuable for their next career."
- "In Asia conferences become a venue for people to take a day off, enjoy food, and relax."
- "No wonder people can't find the value if they do actually take away a memorable experience as well as some crucial learning."

Discouragements:
- "We are just happy that people don't complain when they leave."
- "I'm just looking for some good tips for making conference attendees still engaged in the afternoon sessions."
- "This industry is dying. I am considering retraining to see where I can start a new career."

Skepticism:
- "I don't use social media in the same way I view door-to-door sales, something of an invasion of privacy."
- "There are probably conferences on Facebook. However, all of them are probably just doing similar things and pushing out information that already exists on their website."

- "The ultimate goal is the bottom line. I couldn't get there. Maybe because I don't understand the challenges we are faced with."

Search for new solutions:
- "I think it's down to us organizers to try some new invention."
- "My dream is that we can run conferences that delegates will pay out of their own pocket to attend."
- "We have to find new formats for our conferences. There is so much to learn from the other delegates in the room. We are missing something. We have to set up our conferences with this in mind, inspired by what the web has done."

The phrases that come back again and again:
- "I am confused."
- "I don't know what to do."
- "I don't know how to react to what's happening."
- "I don't see the end of the decline."
- "I think there should be a solution."
- "I tried, but spent a lot of time for little results."

On earth, there are two human species. The first takes everything that happens to justify its fears: volcanoes, the bird flu, terrorism, bad weather travel, stock exchange drops, unemployment, taxes, etc.

Is the conference industry permanently in a crisis? No, it's just changing. And it will go on changing...and go on changing.

And if you don't adapt to the changes, you'd better be afraid. For sure you will be impacted.

"The 7 Spells of the new Conference People 2.0" offer a formula for re-inventing yourself as a conference person, a formula that will enable you to have all the skills necessary to not only survive, but to exceed the results of the vast majority of your peers.

The Ingredients

As a magician does with his apprentices, I am now going to describe to you the ingredients we will need for these spells. As most magicians do, I will use ordinary ingredients that you can find around you. I will avoid turtle eyes, crocodile scales, and dove feathers.

I will at the same time introduce the ingredients to you and describe the power you can unleash from them once you know the formula.

We will use three major ingredients.

The Internet

The first one is the Internet.
For sure, you know what it is. For sure, you use it every day.

But I noticed that most conference people are not comfortable with the Internet, holding the misperception that the Internet is responsible for some of the difficulties the convention industry is facing.

I assure you the Internet is your ally.

Search Engines

I am sure you are aware of the search capabilities of Google.

Some years ago, part of the motivation for people to attend a conference was to get information and find out about new trends in their respective markets. Nowadays anyone can get most of that kind of information—and even, in certain cases, more precise information—online. And for old-style conference people this is terrific because one of the major "reasons to buy" becomes obsolete. That's a fact. We just have to adapt ourselves.

The new "Conference People 2.0" have learned how to use search engines to their benefit. They are able to dominate their industry, given that any person searching for the main topics within their market can find them using search engines and perusing just the first page of results. We all know that being on Google means being on the first page or nothing. Do you know that less than 80 percent of people searching on Google don't go to the second page of results?

So your conference had better be on the first page and among the first results displayed.

Sure, you can spend money for paid sponsored links on Google. But it will cost you money and have less impact than what you can get with what is called "natural rank-ing." Google works with algorithms, meaning programs that are precise and conduct searches using the same process. Sometimes Google changes the rules of its algorithms, but we, as experts, are watching and immediately adjust our strategies to the new guidelines. That means the power of search engines that makes you fear a decline in attendees can also serve as a powerful tool to get new customers.

The Successful Conference team has developed the "Conference Sales System" that they implement for you so that, in a matter of weeks, you can reach the first page of

Google search results and attain even a first position, which gives you ultimate exposure when someone in your industry searches for one of the major topics or issues he or she may have.

"Conference People 2.0" use the search engines to their benefit. In setting up this automated selling machine that runs 24/7, they have access to permanent new leads and achieve a high rate of success in sales conversion.

Forums and Blogs

Forums are also considered a threat by old-minded conference professionals in that they serve as competitors and can reduce the number of potential participants to an event. Certainly, some forums bring very valuable information to your customers about trends as well as effective solutions to their problems.

There is a high probability that top-quality blogs exist in your market too. Any author, speaker, or personality who understands how to make his or her message reach the maximum number of persons is now running a blog. This is the power of the new content-generated web. I am sure that you are aware of all the forums and reference blogs or information websites in your industry.

For "Conference People 2.0," forums and blogs become a rich source of information. Spell # 1 ("Tell me the hottest topics for my industry") will instruct you in two easy-to-implement, time-saving ways to automate the process of identifying your competition and search out upcoming trends in your market online.

Virtual Event Technologies

There is a commonly held anxiety about the advent of virtual events. Many of us as conference people are afraid that they will replace our real-life conferences. In fact, these emerging virtual technologies can empower you as real-life conference people rather than serve as a threat.

First, let's address the case against virtual events. Some say that these are a big threat to conventions. I say, "B.S."

Virtual event technologies are a great invention. But they are only an "event technology," meaning that essentially these pure virtual events are not detrimental to the conference industry per se. These events may bother some small conferences or take a small portion of your customers, but they will not affect the core of your clients. They are not diverting the most interesting ones, both intellectually and financially. So you don't need to worry.

On the contrary, integrating these technologies into your real-life event gives you a new dimension and a capability to gain more new customers than you might have lost because of this technology.

Some months ago, experts were speaking about hybrid events. Wrong definition. Wrong concept.

The good news is that there are only two categories of events, the first being pure virtual events, the second, real life conferences. There are no hybrid events, only real life conferences that will increasingly integrate virtual event technologies. Virtual technologies open up the door for you to generate additional sources of revenues.

The pure virtual events, insofar as there is no total and permanent obstacle to travel, will remain a niche. The existing technologies now and in the next five years cannot replace the Denver Auto Show where you sit and smell the leather interior of the new concept cars, a CES in Las Vegas where you touch every new electronic device, or an Equitana Horse World Show where you can touch, smell, and ride the most exclusive horses in the world.

I am a technology defender and addict. Because I used to work in the artificial intelligence area for Internet platforms (i.e. at the cutting edge of what the Internet can provide), I think I know precisely what technology is able to do for now and, for that matter, for the next three to four years. And it is an acknowledged fact that current technology is unable to offer the same kind of services that a 50,000-attendee horse or car trade show can do.

This fear is for those who love to flagellate themselves. Would you want to make a multi-million dollar deal on a virtual event? There is simply no direct substitution for real-life events at the moment—unless you know how to do the Star Trek stunt of "Beam me up, Scotty."

So the good news is that virtual event technology will be used by real-life conferences and become a source of additional services and revenues. This is part of Spell #4 and will be revealed later.

Another benefit of real-life conferences is to cut participants off from their day-to-day worries and to gain some perspective on the situation, which they cannot have while attending a virtual event from their office. This is an asset to promoting your conference.

Social Media

Social media serves, in essence, as a technological replica of conferences. Both offer powerful ways to help people meet the right people who can bring solutions to them. The first ones are automated, impersonal at first glance, while the others are full, hand-made, and defend themselves as bringing the "true" opportunities of "real meetings."

All of this is both true and false. You can build real, deep relationships using social media, and you can attend a real-world conference and connect with nobody.

What "Conference People 2.0" realize is that both are similar in nature. They are both tools for getting answers and provide help for our jobs or careers.

The results we get with one or the other come from the way we use them. It is all about knowing what to do with each of them and what to expect from them.

The difficulty with social media offerings is that they represent such a vast expanse of technologies that it is very easy to get lost and not know what to do with them.

To make things more complicated, although they have found a common name under social media, they are all different in terms of their technical features and in regard to inside rules and etiquette. Moreover, a conference person must adjust his or her mindset in order to use each one effectively.

In addition to this, all conferences are not equal. What works for a bankers' conference is not the same as what works for an electronic music DJs' conference. That's the reason why the research department of Successful Conference has tested and then stratified the social media strategies that bring results for each category of event. Therefore every training program and every "done-for-you" system is customized for the specific event each customer is organizing.

As a result of all these experiences, each type of conference can now take tremendous profits from social media—from all of them: Linkedin, Twitter, and even Facebook—thanks to a new breakthrough that our studies confirmed a few months ago and that you will discover in Chapter 4.

NLP—Neuro Linguistic Programming

Neuro Linguistic Programming is an insufficiently used approach in our industry. It includes a bunch of efficient techniques to manage organizational changes and customer psychology, based on "a model of interpersonal communication" chiefly concerned with the relationship between successful patterns of behavior and the identification and understanding of repetitive patterns of thoughts among clients or one's team.

This is a system that seeks to make people more self-aware and educate them in effective communication in order to change their patterns of mental and emotional behavior. Applied to sales and business relationships, NLP is an incredibly powerful tool that enables people to unblock the structures of human communication and human excellence. By doing so people can think, communicate, and manage themselves and others more effectively.

Successful Conference has developed a specific "Conference Personal Coaching Program" designed to solve the day-to-day challenges of conference persons, such as being able to deal with:

- the stress of having everything done on time
- the pressure of having so many details to check up on
- interpersonal relationships when delegating under pressure to on-site people who may have little motivation
- maintaining a positive attitude and able to broadcast to the team the energy necessary to make it happen
- time management while multitasking
- restoring harmony between a stressful, often far-from-home job and family life
- instant decision making
- all other psychological challenges connected to our exciting but demanding conference jobs

Your magician discovered NLP principles fifteen years ago, thanks to the master of NLP: Anthony Robbins. Your magician followed the entire curriculum the latter offered until he became an NLP master trainer himself. He recommends the book *The Unlimited Power* for those who want a complete overview of what this science can bring to them, both in their personal and professional lives.

In the "7 Spells of the New Conference People 2.0" as well as in all Successful Conference training programs, you will be able to get what you need when making conference preparations so that your day-to-day life is easier and your approach to planning is more efficient.

NLP is the ingredient you will learn how to use for Spell #7 (Give me the power to stay on top and turn the stress away on demand).

Now we have all that we need to start our course on magic.

Spell by spell, you will understand how you can (yes, you can), in the next months, acquire these skills and implement them in your daily job so that your next conference will be the most successful conference you ever imagined.

Chapter 3
Spell # 1: Reveal the Hottest Topics for my Industry

The Hottest Topics are at your Fingertips

Included here is some instruction on the basic use of Internet, blogs, and forums. You will regard them all as allies before the end of this chapter.

The hottest topics for your industry already are engraved in the Internet.

The success of Spell #1 is not so much in the "how to" as in the "how to make it last."

This means that there are two parts to the learning:
- the first examines where the hottest topics are and how to find them
- the second illustrates how to get alerted when new ones appear and how to follow-up on them

It is all about mapping your industry sources of information. I am not speaking about the big corporate websites. I am speaking about the "underground" ones, where trends are identified before everybody knows them.

Here is a step-by-step guide to finding them.

IMPORTANT NOTICE REGARDING TRAINING INCLUDED IN THIS BOOK:
Before you start this first training, please be sure that you have at least one hour available. The efficiency of this training depends on your focus and being able to go until

the end of the process without being interrupted. Do not dash this exercise off. It is crucial. It may take one hour or more, but the distinctions or breakthroughs that you will acquire are worth more than one hour of your time

Training 1: How to Find the Hottest Topics in my Industry

1. Take a blank sheet of paper and write down the ten most important topics that you think people are concerned about in your industry. You can do this in a bullet-point format or in plain text, whatever is most convenient for you.
2. Sort them from the most important one to the least important one.
3. Take another sheet of paper and, in a bullet-point format, try to convert these ten most important topics into ten lines of keywords (each line must not have more than three words). These are the terms that those people belonging to your market enter in the Google search box.
4. Once you get these ten lines of keywords (with a maximum of three words per line), go to Google, and for each line of keywords do the following:
a. Enter the one to three keywords in the Google search box and click on search.
b. Google will display just beneath the search box the number of results related to this search. Note the number. It will give you the factual ranking of your ten searches, which may be different from the ranking that you did a few minutes ago, according to your personal experience. This number is pure statistics, meaning it is a perfect representation of the real concerns of your market.
c. Read the lines of each result. Some of them will remind you that you forgot an important topic. Add

this topic on your first page as topic #11, then #12, etc.

Don't stop on the first page, which usually displays ten results only. Click on the next button and go at least until page ten so that you go through the first one hundred results related to your topic.

d. While doing this exercise you will see the websites, the blogs, the forums, the individuals who are the rainmakers on the Internet for your industry. Take a blank sheet of paper and write down their names and the URL of their websites. You may discover then that some of them have a power of influence that you hadn't imagined before. You will use this list of influencers later for another spell.

e. When you have finished, go back to the new lines that you have added from topic #1 to topic #10 and do the same.

Training 2: How to Find the Hottest Sources of Information in my Industry

1. Take the sheet of paper where you wrote down the names of influencers, blogs, and individuals that you noticed during the previous training.

2. Go on Google and for each of your #1 to #10 topics, using your one to three keywords, search for:
    o *Blog: YourMainKeywords*
    o *YourMainKeywords "powered by wordpress"*
    o *YourMainKeywords "wordpress"*
    o *Forum: YourMainKeywords*
    o *News: YourMainKeywords*
    o *Trends: YourMainKeyword*

3. Don't stop on page one, which usually displays ten results only. Click on the next button and go at

least until page ten so that you go through the first one hundred results related to your search.

4.   Use the following blank page, and when you have finished, you now have a precise list of where the information starts.

Now imagine that each member of your team has the discipline to do this exercise even once a quarter, and you could share the data each of you have gathered every month. Can you imagine the richness of this information? You already have one-twelfth of the power of Spell#1!

Spell #1 Magic Word: KEYWORDS

Mastering Spell #1: How to Make the Hottest Topics and Trends Come to You

When you master Spell#1 at full strength:
- You will use for your benefit what is called the "user-content-generated web" at no cost.
- You will receive directly in your e-mail new emerging trends on your market.
- You will automate the process of getting the hottest topics in your industry.
- You will create a permanent spying dashboard. Each time you open it, it will tell you within five minutes what has to be taken into consideration for your industry.

…and much more.

It will take you only two weeks to master the advanced, fully detailed strategies included in the comprehensive "Conference Production System" from Successful Conference, which comes with comprehensive guidelines and step-by-step worksheets.

Chapter 4
Spell #2: Attract the Most Outstanding Speakers

How to Identify the Best Speakers for your next Conference

There are three parts to mastering this spell:
-       How to identify the best speakers for your next conference
-       How to engage in conversation with them and make them appreciate you
-       How to transform them into fans so that they will "beg" you to let them speak at your conference

From the Internet

You already did the biggest part of the research work while preparing your Spell#1. Go back to the worksheet where you wrote down the individual influencers while doing your industry mapping.

From Social Media

Influencers are people who reach a great number of people. Let's forget old-fashioned influencers and speak about those who count and will count in your industry. They have no choice but to use social media, and therefore you will find most of them on Linkedin, Facebook, and Twitter.

Explaining what Twitter does, how to use it for your conference, and how to get results from it is the focus of a complete eight-week program called "Conference Advanced Twitter Program." I encourage you to make a search like "Twitter for beginners" on the Internet if you are a beginner.

In fact, there is only one thing you have to know to do the following training: Twitter is the most powerful tool for broadcasting small bits of information to masses in a second. For this reason, any person having a goal to influence a market goes there.

In addition to that, everything in Twitter is measurable. It is easy to get a ranking of people according to their broadcasting power. We will later see how to judge the quality of their messages or, more importantly, the responsiveness of their audience. At the moment, we will only find the most powerful ones.

Training 3: How to Find the Best Speakers for your Industry on Twitter

1. Go on the web and type in the following URL http://www.twellow.com
2. In the search box enter the name of your industry and click on the search button. This is pure magic: you get all the influencers of your industry using Twitter ranked by the greatest number of people following them, meaning those interested in receiving their message each time they send a new one. This number is just beside the label "followers." You also get the city and country where they are located, which could help you discover someone from abroad capable of influencing your market.
3. If you click on the name of this person, you will access his or her profile and see all the messages that he or she has sent previously.
4. On the right side of the profile screen you should see the URL of his or her website where you can go to explore further. If you are already using Twitter and have an account, then Twellow will allow you to immediately follow this person by clicking on

the "follow" button, meaning that you will receive every message he or she sends in real time.

Training 4: How to Find the Best Speakers for your Industry on Google

Google has developed specific searches to find people who say they are experts in a specific area on Twitter. It is not the purpose of this training to explain to you the subtitles of Google's specific searches that directly speak to its algorithms, but there is a very technical type of search that will dig into your experts' biographies in Twitter and retrieve for you the famous ones. You just need to do the following:

1. Take the sheet of paper where you have listed your influencers.
2. Take the sheet of paper with your keywords.
3. For each of your keywords line, enter exactly this in the Google search box:
   intext:"bio * YourKeywords" site:twitter.com

Training 5: How to Find the Advanced Influencers of your Industry by their Websites

A real influencer should have a website or blog. A real influencer wanting to get reached on the Internet should have told his or her webmaster to have his or her name in the title of the pages of any website or blog about him or her. Google has developed specific searches specifically focusing on the title of websites and blogs pages.

1. Take the sheet of paper where you have listed your influencers.
2. Take the sheet of paper with your keywords.
3. For each of your keywords line, enter exactly this in the Google search box:
   allintitle: YourKeywords

Training 6: How to Find the Emerging Influencers Wanting to Lead your Industry

A real influencer thinks about attracting people related to what is most important for your industry. That means that smart people will build their Twitter name using the most common keywords of your industry.

1.   Take the sheet of paper with your keywords.
2.   Take the sheet of paper where you have listed your influencers.
3.   For each of your keywords line, enter exactly this in the Google search box:
        intitle:"*YourKeywords* * on twitter" site:twitter.com

Seven advanced strategies to identify your potential best speakers using Facebook, Linkedin, and Twitter are detailed in the "Conference Professional Force Program."

How to Engage in Conversation with your Targeted Speakers and make them Appreciate you

There are specific strategies for conference producers to engage in conversation with potential best speakers for each social media. They are different depending on whether you are on Linkedin, Facebook, or Twitter.

The individuals that you have just identified may be on one or another of these social media. If they are on all three of them, this is a good clue that they have in mind to become an important source of broadcasting in your industry.

Training 7: How to Engage in Conversation with your Targeted Speakers on Facebook

For the purpose of this training, let's focus on those who are on Facebook. Explaining what Facebook does, how to use it for your conference, and how to get results is illustrated in a complete eight-week program called "Conference Advanced Facebook Program." I encourage you to make a search such as "Facebook for beginners" on the Internet if you are a beginner. But there is only one thing you have to know to do the following training: your influencer can exist on Facebook either as an individual, with a personal profile, or as a brand on what Facebook calls a "business page," or on both. No need to say that those who have their own "business page" intend to exert more influence.

1. Open your Facebook account.
2. For each of the influencers you have identified, enter their complete name in the Facebook search box.
3. You will have a better view if you click on the link "Get more results" so that Facebook will allow you to get results within "people" or within "pages."
4. Take the list of your targeted influencers and write down the URLs of their Facebook profiles and/or their Facebook business pages.
5. Do not invite them as friends now! This is the biggest mistake you can make, given that they don't know you.
6. Read what they post on their walls (profile and/or business pages).
7. See how people react and comment on what they post.
8. If they or somebody commenting asks a question that you have an answer to, start the conversation by adding your value in the comment section. Do not sell anything; do not do anything else that adds value to the current conversation, without pushing you or your product. Act as if you are entering a cocktail party. You hear a conversation

where you can add some value, and you add it. Period.

9. Come back every two days and do the same, if applicable. Maybe you will have the opportunity to enter the conversation only after two weeks of watching. That will be the moment. Do not push. Don't be in a hurry. The time will come.

10. After two or three positive interactions, with you having added value to the conversation on the wall of your targeted influencers, you already have a real probability that THEY have answered you or sent you a thank you message, or even provided you with a friend request. Bingo.

11. If not, keep on adding value. Then after five or six interactions on your part, just send them a private message congratulating them on the role they have in the community, for the specific information they gave, or for the special help they gave to a person commenting, etc. Be sincere in your private message and try to add value at the same time. Don't do this on the public wall!

12. There is a high probability that your targeted influencer will answer privately to your message. And half a chance that you will get a friend invitation from him or her at the same time. Bingo.

13. In case you receive an answer without a friend request, it is now obvious and natural for you to reply with a friend request as a thank you. Bingo.

14. You know your job. It is now easy for you to go cautiously but deeper into the relationship until you find the exact moment when you can suggest that he or she might speak at your conference if this has not come from him or her first. Bingo.

Spell #2 Magic Word: GIVE

Mastering Spell #2: How to Transform your Targeted Speakers into Fans

When you master Spell#2 at full strength:

You will be able to propel your targeted speakers on the Internet in a way that:

- o does not require more than a few hours of their time
- o dramatically enhances their reputation on the Internet
- o propels them on the Internet search engine.

This is the ultimate win-win program that will make them respect you, need you, and beg you to speak at your conference, on your conditions.

…and much more.

The Successful Conference experts will work for you, as they will set up their search engines and social media propelling technology for your dream speakers.

Using these advanced strategies included in the efficient "Conference Speakers System" from Successful Conference, none of your targeted speakers can afford to reject your offer. They will beg to speak at your conference, and you will have the dominant position for the negotiation.

Chapter 5
Spell #3: Enable my Next Conference to be Sold Out

It has Never Been so Easy to Sell Conferences

Most of our conference customers complain about the growing difficulties in selling their event. Not only do they sell less easily, but they also sell later, increasing the stress of having a negative balance sheet at the end.

It is a reality that most of them have online registration capabilities. You have them, don't you? If not, please stop reading this book and call your webmaster or a consulting company to set up this must-have sales channel.

What surprised me in the last survey we did is the still high proportion of sales relying on salespersons working over the phone, using the old method of "cold-calling." I wouldn't suggest ending that sales channel right away, but I would definitely recommend that you start using the new sales channel built on the power of the Internet.

There are two ways the Internet and social media can dramatically boost your sales.

How to Transform your Existing Customers into Effective Salespersons for your Conference

The basic way to multiply sales for your event is to use existing customers to sell for you.

Remember that this is a fundamental of social media: spreading the world within a community.

Here is a powerful way to do this using Facebook.

I hear some of you thinking "Facebook is not for me. Facebook is not for business."

Let's talk about that…

Is Facebook for your Conference?

There are a lot of myths and legends about Facebook. The biggest one is summarized in these two preconceptions:
-    Facebook is for friends
-    Facebook is not for business

Facebook is for Friends
This is not a myth. This is true.

Facebook means:
-    Relaxing
-    Discovery
-    Spare time
-    No stress
-    Conviviality
-    No worries
-    You are casual, in underwear
-    You have a drink nearby
-    You have music in the background

Facebook is not for Business.
This is a myth. The truth is:

Facebook means:
- NO SELLING
- NO HARD SELLING
- NO SOLLICITATION
- NO SALES PITCH
- NO BUSINESS CARD or TRADE
- You are not in a suit
- You don't wear a tie
- You don't wear shoes

In order for you to understand for yourself what Facebook can do for your conference, let's go to your favorite bar or restaurant with cool music and a lounge atmosphere. Let's listen to the conversation of the two guys at the table nearby. They are sharing a drink, laughing, telling each other about their last vacations.

Here is the conversation:

-Wow, Jeff. Your vacation was great. I'd like to go there too. I cannot believe you did not call the office or work during that week! It's not you!
-Mmmm. Ya. I was just connected to my Facebook for fun. In fact, I just remembered one thing. I saw on one of my friends' newsfeeds that he was impressed by a free report about our industry. I clicked on the link and started to read it. Was so intense that I read the twenty pages in one shot. This report described a new way to solve the major problem I have with our marketing return on investment. They described precisely how to increase conversion rates. It was so amazing that I called my assistant to test it while I was on the beach. She did. And you know what?

- Tell me...
- Plus ten percent in one week.
- Really?
-Yes. We will extend the test period to two other weeks and then I think we will switch to that provider.
- Wow. It seems powerful. You know I have the same problem too. Can you give me the website URL so that I can see that myself?
-Yes, you can find the link on my Facebook wall.
- Cool. I'll go there just after our drink. Do you want another one? By the way, how is Suzy doing? Does she still go to her painting lessons?

What do you think happened afterwards?

The first thing Paul did when he returned home was to:
-       open his Facebook
-       go on his friend's newsfeeds
-       click on the link
-       download the free report
-       read it...and...test it too!

Is this business?
Sure!
Absolutely!

Is this a way of selling?
Yes! And more powerful in terms of conversion than a sales meeting. The beauty is that they are not face-to-face with a salesperson. They are not being sold. They are buying. They are controlling the process.

That's what Facebook can do for your conference.

Using your Facebook Page to Transform your Existing Customers into Effective Salespersons for your Conference

Once again, it is not the purpose of this book to explain to you what Facebook does, how to use it for your conference, or how to get results. For the following training, there is only one thing you have to know: why a Facebook page, if you know how to use it properly, is such a "viral" tool for selling your event.

A Facebook page is a specific page that you can easily create and that will be dedicated to your conference only. In that sense, this page will be totally different and autonomous from your personal Facebook profile where you communicate with your friends. On this Facebook page, you will provide valuable information regarding your conference. An effective Facebook page strategy contains the precise answers to these crucial questions:
-      Which content to provide
-      Which frequency
-      Which media support
-      Which interactivity

The responses to these vary from one event to another. This is the reason why the step-by-step guidelines that you follow in the "Conference Promotion System" will ensure that you set up the strategy that will bring the greatest results for your conference.

The purpose of this chapter is to illustrate how a Facebook page can sell for you. It emphasizes the need to create your page according to the specifications put forth and as quickly as possible before your competitors have the chance to do so. If you fail to take immediate action, you risk losing a leading position in your market.

So let me explain to you how a Facebook page works. For the purpose of this example, let's say a person named Peter Schmidt has just created a Facebook page dedicated to his banking conference, which he has named "the future of banking."

On top of each Facebook page is a "like" button. People need to click on this button to interact with Peter Schmidt's page. If you give people a compelling reason to join your page (we will get to that later), they will click on the "like" button and...

ALL their friends will see in the newsfeeds that Peter Schmidt likes "the future of banking" page, with a link to his page.

Do you think there are other bankers among Peter Schmidt's friends?
Is he is one of them? Sure.

What do you think one of his banker friends, upon seeing that Peter Schmidt likes "the future of banking page" on his own Facebook newsfeeds, will do?

He will click on the link to see what his friend likes, won't he? Surveys show that 41 percent of Facebook users click to know what a friend of theirs says he or she likes.

So this banker friend of Peter Schmidt will:
- click on the link
- arrive on his Facebook page
- see the "like" button
- click on it to see more

And...what happens?

Their friends will see this in their newsfeeds.

Do you think this second banker has bankers as friends too?

Sure...

That's the viral process. It is technical, based on this powerful Facebook feature, and psychological, based on friends' interactions. There is one key point that could make or break your "viral" success with this strategy: the name of your Facebook page. This is the reason why we will undertake specific training to be sure you have this key element mastered.

Having your Facebook Page Working Virally for your Conference

Training 8: How to Choose the Name of your Facebook Page for Viral Attraction

1. Before everything, avoid the common mistake of taking your brand name.
2. Choose a generic name that describes best what everybody in your industry is waiting for.
3. Why not your name? Let's assume you are organizing a conference for bankers, and you are proud of your name: COFUBANK2012. That means "conference on the future of banking 2012." Cool name! You have two choices. You can name your Facebook page:
    - cofubank or
    - the future of banking

What's the best?

We all have an ego and want our brand name to be used as often as possible, but this will make the difference between a Facebook page that stagnates at one hundred and a Facebook page that rockets to thousands or much more.

Here is why: Let's say you made the mistake of calling your Facebook page "COFUBANK2012." Who may "like" and become a fan of your page?

§ to find you, people must know you (cannot invent cofubank)

§ to have a reason to join, they must have registered first (so they must already be clients, and what you need to attract are new prospects)

§ even the person who is already a customer may not find a compelling reason to join your Facebook page. If your conference main site is well designed, all the information the person needs is on your website, isn't it? So why go to your Facebook page?

That's the reason why you absolutely need to choose a generic name that describes best what everybody in your industry is waiting for if you want to trigger the viral effect.

All the people in your industry will be touched by the title of your page first and then by the content you release to them.

Identifying which content and a compelling reason to join your Facebook page are specific tasks to perform before transforming your page into a news hub for your industry.

Here are some tips that will give you the will to go further:

- "Click here to receive updates from the (blank) industry major experts."

- "Click here to discover the hot new topics preview" or "Click here to get instant access to a free report about (blank)."

Using your Facebook Page to Dominate your Market with your Conference

Before we enter this important section about how to dominate your market with Facebook, it is important to be sure that you are convinced about what a Facebook page can do for your event.

If you are not still convinced, here is what it will do for your conference:
- all the people that click on the "like" button will receive newsfeeds
- all that you publish on your page will appear in real time
- each time viewers like something you post, their friends will see it ("Paul Schmidt likes your page" with a link to your page)
- each time viewers comment on something you post, their friends will see it ("Paul Schmidt commented blah-blah-blah" with a link to your page)
- and we'll see more later

Not convinced?

Remember the name of the game is to capture the "cool" aspect of your whole industry. "The future of banking" is designed to capture bankers. Aren't they your prospects? But this first part is enough to make you understand how crucial it is for you to be on Facebook and to capture your market. You have seen how easy it is for someone who is able to master the way professionals interact on Facebook.

The only question is:
Who will capture your market? You—or someone else?

The first will be the winner.

And you will be able to take advantage of the viral nature not only of Facebook but also of Linkedin and Twitter for your conference. It will take four weeks with the "Conference Promotion System" for you to develop the expertise to align the offerings of the three major social media sites with your conference strategy. You will extend your power in your industry and attract a lot of new prospects.

Now you will be able to dominate your market using social media with the "Conference Promotion System."

How to Transform your Exhibitors and Sponsors into Effective Salespersons for your Conference

The aim of any exhibitor who has bought exhibition space from you is to have the maximum number of visitors at his or her booth. The aim of any sponsor that has set up a sponsorship operation with you is to have the maximum number of visitors participate.

Correspondingly, your job is to provide both with any additional services that maximize their return on investment.

You have already understood in reading this book the power of social media to increase the number of visitors at your conference. Up to now we have just used this tool to draw customers and prospects. Now just imagine if each of your exhibitors and sponsors were to do the same and use the same social media force to bring new participants to your event!

You might be able to multiply the effect your exhibitors and sponsors have for attracting their customers and prospects to your conference. In the "Conference Sales System," we provide our customers with a turnkey kit, which they can send complementarily to each of their exhibitors and prospects.

It is all about "Return of Investment": ROI.

The "Maximize your Exhibition ROI—Kit" and "Maximize your Sponsorship ROI—Kit," which we customize for your conference, contain:
- a step-by-step guide for your exhibitor or sponsor to use his or her existing social media or list to direct customers and prospects to your conference, including
  o a chapter using Linkedin
  o a chapter using Facebook
  o a chapter using Twitter
  o a chapter using your exhibitor or sponsor's blog

Imagine the results regarding your conference in terms of bottom line.

A New Additional Service to Boost your Sales in Terms of Exhibition Space and Sponsorships

We love to speak about the "double effect" of the "Maximize your Exhibition ROI—Kit" and "Maximize your Sponsorship ROI—Kit" for your sales force. These are powerful and efficient sales tools that are:

- a proof of excellence from you as a conference organizer

- an effective way to make sure your exhibitors or sponsors are confident that buying from you is good for their bottom line.

The feedback we get from conference sales people who use these turnkey kits indicates that it changes the way their prospects think. The moment they understand that they can themselves take part in the promotion of the exhibition or connect with the sponsor they have bought from you, they are immediately engaged and it becomes their "thing." They become instantly more involved, and the sales conversion increases dramatically.

Generating new Leads with Virtual Event Technologies

Virtual events being cheaper, they can attract people who wouldn't have registered for your main conference and then become hot prospects for your next real-life events further on. This represents an additional port of entry for your sales.

Mastering Spell #3: How to Create an Automated Selling Machine for your Conference that Brings you new Prospects and Converts them 24/7

Are you Missing the Chance of Using new Available Sales Channels for Conferences?

Many industries have already integrated automated sales funnels in their processes. Gap, Ralph Lauren, Disney, Barnes and Noble, Nike, Blockbuster, and American Apparel are all among the top e-retailers for 2009—although their primary source of business comes from real life.

Gap sells through its traditional sales channel from 8 a.m. to 8 p.m. all over the world, staffed with pleasant and welcoming salespersons. Gap also sells 24/7/52 on their website associated with their social media and search engine strategies.

The new "Conference People 2.0" rely on the power of the Internet for building a system that works by itself 24 hours a day, 7 days a week, 52 weeks a year. The beauty of this is that once it is set up, it permanently brings to you new prospects with little maintenance.

Let's forget for a few moments about "organizing" and focus on your prospect side. Let's step into the prospect's shoes and feel what he or she feels when hearing about your event.

The paradox in organizing an event is that although the event usually lasts only a few days and is supposed to create a certain momentum, the sales process usually lacks momentum.

Because people know on which date your event will happen—let's say in eight months—they know that they have eight months to register. Early bird discounts may smooth this sales routine, but event organizers are usually so focused on the final event that they are far from being permanently focused on sales.

How to Automate the Process of Selling your Conference

Building an automated sales machine specifically for your conference needs to set up an increasing momentum, guiding your prospect through a process where the probability of signing with you is high.

In fact, the "Conference Sales System" will build three automated sales machines: one for registrations from attendees, one for sponsorship, and one for exhibition sales.

The automation includes three phases:
1. Attention
2. Momentum
3. Conversion

Grabbing your Prospects' Attention

The first goal is to grab the attention of your prospects and to make your conference important for them. You may have a mailing program to solicit registrations with your previous clients; therefore, you know that the conversion rate of an e-mailing campaign is very low.

Because your prospects are, like you, busy and over-solicited, some of your messages will end up in their e-mail spam box. Or they may see your e-mail, but because they know that your next event is in eight months, they will have no urgency to act. They may even not open the e-mail.

People tend to pay less and less attention to the e-mails they receive…unless…they are waiting for them.
Here is the secret of the attention part of the conference sales system…

The way to grab your prospects' attention is to issue a sequence of messages that initiate the relationship and interest so that they expect the unfolding of your story and the valuable content you are providing to them. And this leads them smoothly to the second part of the "Conference Sales System."

Automating the Sales Funnel Momentum

Marketers know that the average business prospects require six to seven exposures prior to any buying action. This is the power of pre-programming, which is included in your "Conference Sales System," which is fully customized to your conference and your industry.

Pre-programming captures the attention of your potential prospects through the huge noise of messages they receive. And your messages are picked out and read before and/or instead of others. This is the best way to pull them, to attract them into your registration or sales process.

The prospects, as usual, won't receive an e-mail requesting registration, but you might find them engaged in a real conversation, following a story that brings them valuable content through the "Conference Sales System" process. Moreover, they pay attention to the conversation because they remain engaged in it until the third part of the sales system: conversion.

Automating the 24/7 Conversion

This conversation guides your prospect until he or she takes action and decides to buy. You are now able to create sales accelerators three to four times a year, when you need them.

Here is what the "Conference Sales System" does:
-    It transforms the way your prospects think about your conference.
-    It changes their mindset from "What if I buy? What if I register?" to "I must buy now. I must register now."

- It determines for you the two best periods to gather new registrations, new sponsorships, and exhibition sales.

At that point, you will know which offer is the most powerful for your conference to create virtual scarcity, and you will have your prospects make their decision now.

The success is in the sequence and in the automated selling machine. The beauty of the program is that once it is up and running, it works by itself, bringing revenues and customers to you.

One additional consequence of having set up your "Conference Sales System" is that your conference will appear in the highest position on the search engine for your prospects searching the major topics of your industry.

This is one of the "snowball effects" of your "Conference Sales System" using Internet power to increase your sales and profits.

Another consequence that also accelerates your sales is that the combination of momentum and conversion allows you to increase profits by up selling with additional services that you did not even know your prospects wanted.

As a result of the implementation of such an automated sales funnel, you will decide by yourself, and earlier than you imagined, to substitute this new channel for the "grandfather" one.

If you yourself are a telesales for the convention industry, I have good news for you. You can take advantage of a great retraining opportunity and switch from a difficult and stressful job to a new one, which every conference is begging for: people who know how to set up an automated sales funnel for their event.

And as this is your current job, you will be the best positioned to build the most effective process for them. There is not only an important need for conference professionals who can implement automated sales processes, but also for trainers who can generate new people ready to implement them. You can study how to master these skills yourself or get assistance by e-mailing your request to certifications@successfulconference.com. So if you are a sales person in the convention industry, this is your time to act.

When you master Spell #3 at full strength:
-       You will benefit from our technology for your three major customer segments:
o   one automated sales funnel for selling new registrations
o   one automated sales funnel for selling new exhibition spaces
o   one automated sales funnel for selling new sponsorships

Spell #3 Magic Word: SOCIAL MEDIA

ক∞ও

Chapter 6
Spell #4: Add Significant Revenues to my next Conference

Conferences and Social Media are Twins

The value behind conference organization is to help people meet the right person who can make their professional life easier. This is our permanent goal as conference people.

If you stay in the traditional conference world, brainstorming how to generate additional revenues means searching for new ways to help your participants find what they are looking for more easily, more efficiently, and—ultimate benefit -, while spending a memorable moment.

What do you think the value behind social media is?

Exactly the same: helping people meet other people of interest.

What's exciting is that social media, just to speak about the three major ones (Facebook, Linkedin, and Twitter), have a vast list of specific features for connecting people. And as it is now the center of Internet technology, engineers are inventing new connecting social media features every day.

For us, as "Conference People 2.0," that means that every day, new ways of bringing core value to our customers are available through new social media features. Amazing, isn't it?

The "Conference Sales System" includes twelve powerful new strategies especially developed for conferences based on new services with high value that will generate new revenues for your event. Among these is an ironical one, whereby conferences take their revenge on their "supposed" enemy: the virtual events.

How to Overcome the Biggest Fears Conference Organizers Have

The biggest threats that most conference organizers say they have or will have to face in the very near future are:

-    Decisions to buy (registrations, exhibition space, and sponsorships) are made later and later, increasing the pressure on the conference bottom line.
-    Companies tend to shorten the stay of their staff when allowing them to attend real-life events.
-    As a result, conference producers tend to reduce the length of their events, making it difficult to maintain the same level of pricing.

Accepting these trends as given facts, we have searched for replacement solutions not only to keep revenues at the same level, but also to upgrade them. This is what we call "the revenge of real-life conferences against virtual events." In a few minutes, you will stop perceiving these technologies as a direct threat to live events.

The Revenge of Real-life Conferences Against Virtual Events

Training 9: Generating Additional Revenues from Virtual Event Technologies

Virtual conferencing technologies allow people to connect on a website where they have access to speakers' sessions. The available content can be:
- full real-time video streaming, which is the closest to the real world event experience
- catch-up videos of the sessions
- PowerPoint presentations
- PDF summaries
- extracts

For every conference, there are people who follow what you do, but for one reason or another could not attend your event. This could be for personal, financial, timing, vacation reasons, etc. But these people are still interested in the content that has been delivered during your conference. That is the reason why, if you don't do it already, you MUST invest in a professional multi-media team, which you can hire just for the event and post-event period, with the precise mission to:
- record everything
- produce everything in as many formats as possible

Every forty-five-minute session can be transformed into:

- a forty-five-minute full real-time video streaming
- a forty-five-minute catch-up video
- three fifteen-minute videos for each sub-topic
- nine five-minute straight-to-the-point videos
- a forty-five-minute full audio version of the session
- three fifteen-minute audio versions for each sub-topic

- nine five-minute straight-to-the-point audio versions
- one complete PowerPoint presentation
- three partial PowerPoint presentations for each topic
- nine straight-to-the-point PowerPoint presentations
- one full PDF of written full transcript of the session
- three partial PDFs of written transcript for each topic
- nine straight-to-the-point PDFs of written transcripts
- PDF summaries
- extracts

Why so many supports?
- Because each of them has value.
- Because each of them can become part of a new product or service with value for the people who missed the sessions.
- Because social media and search engines provide so many different ways of making money with different formats that it is cheap to generate profits you are passing by.
- Because we are in the era of multi-media and multi-consumption.
- Because the way of "consuming conferences" evolves—just as you can decide to use your landline or mobile phone to reach someone or to send a text message or to Skype. Different times, different behaviors, same results.

First, these are sources of additional revenues for acquiring new customers. Second, even participants cannot be everywhere at the same time. They may value access later to sessions they missed. The implementation of all these new sources of revenues is included in the "Conference Sales System," which guides you to build the infrastructure to monetize these valuable materials.

Spell #4 Magic Word: TWINS

Mastering Spell #4: How to Double your Sponsorship Revenues

Sponsorship is closed to partnership, meaning that the best way to visualize a new sponsor's proposal is to listen to and talk with your targeted prospects. They will tell you what they are interested in. Then your job will be to maximize the value of your offer, now aligned with their strategy.

With the advanced strategies included in the impressive "Conference Sponsors System," you will be able to map out all your "sponsorable" assets. You will discover many you hadn't imagined before and master the way to package them in a salable fashion and price them appropriately. The more multi-dimensional your sponsor's proposal is structured, the more chances you have to sell it and to sell it for a high price.

When you master Spell #4 at full strength:
- You will be able to position your "sponsorable" assets as highly valuable packages for your prospects aligned with their strategic priorities
- Build irresistible sponsorship proposals, including stacked-up bottom line-oriented benefits for them
- Identify the right person in your targeted organization who will share your new vision
- Leave room in your proposal for your contact to adjust it to his or her needs and take over your selling process inside his or her company

This is a win-win program, whereby we work closely with you to increase your sponsorship revenues with the goal of doubling them.

Chapter 7
Spell #5: Make my President Happy

The Hidden Power your President can Bring to your Conference

It is all about the synergy between your president and your conference.

We are always surprised how the people in any conference organization are focused on their president during the creation of the event and forget about him or her after some years of operation.

The opposite is also true. How strange it is to notice that presidents are often hands-on for the first event and then just present for the opening dinner or closing cocktail on later occasions.

In most cases, if he or she is the president of your event, this means that he or she has the power, the vision, and the respect from the community your conference is about. This is so valuable that it must be used for each instance of your event.

The president's role is not only to be on stage and to show off, but also to help your team backstage in every stage of your job, from production to promoting.

Training 10: What is the Synergy Between your President and your Conference?

1. Take a blank sheet of paper. Title it "President's Synergy."
2. Divide the sheet of paper in four columns.
3. Title the first column "+."
4. Title the second column "what he/she does."
5. Title the third column "what he/she doesn't do."
6. Title the fourth column "+."
7. Take five to ten minutes to fill in columns 2 and 3.
8. In column 2, write down as it comes to mind all that the president does for your conference—all the help, support, personal commitment, introductions, referees, and facilitations that he or she brings to the table.
9. In column 3, write down as it comes to mind all that you would want the president to do and what he or she does not do.
10. Take a minute or two to verify you haven't forgotten important facts.
11. Then take each point of column 2. In the first column on the left side put a "*" (star) for the points that are the most important for you. Not the ones your president is the more active in, but the ones that, according to you, are more important for your conference and for your job.
12. This is an important part, so please do this classification carefully.
13. Then for each of the points with a "star," in the same first column, write down some ideas or ways that your president could increase his or her actions to help you more. There may be several different ways for the same point. You don't have to evaluate the feasibility at this time. Just write down your wishes.

14. At the same time, you can write down how you can get him or her to do that.
15. Think about a way to increase all the help, support, personal commitment, introductions, referees, and facilitations that he or she brings to the table for your conference.
16. Then take each point from column 3. In the fourth column on the right side put a "*" (star) for the points that are the most important for you. Not the ones your president is less active in, but the ones that, according to you, are more important for your conference and for your job.
17. This is an important part, so please do this classification carefully.
18. Then for each of the points with a "star," in the same fourth column, write down some ideas or ways that your president could increase his/her action to help you more. There may be several different ways for the same point. You don't have to evaluate the feasibility at this time. Just write down your wishes.
19. At the same time, you can write down how you can get him or her to do that.
20. Think about a way to increase all the help, support, personal commitment, introductions, referees, and facilitations that the president brings to the table for your conference.

This should serve as an interesting list of possibilities to make your daily job easier.

Training 11: Does your President have Real Influence?

1. Take a blank sheet of paper. Title it "President's Influence."
2. Divide the sheet of paper into four columns.

3.   Title the first column "Target."

4.   Title the second column "Influence."

5.   Title the third column "Changes."

6.   Title the fourth column "+."

7.   Take five to ten minutes to fill in columns 1 and 2.

8.   In column 1, list the different targets for people that are important for your conference. It could be general targets such as speakers, exhibitors, internal staff, your team, professional organizations, convention centers, etc. or precise individuals who count a lot for your conference, such as Peter Schmidt, if Peter Schmidt is your direct boss.

9.   In column 2, assign a figure from a scale of 0 to 10, where 0 means your president has no influence on this target or individual, and 10 if your president has full influence on this target or individual.

10.   Then for each line, in column 3, write down the figure that you think is possible in terms of influence from your president. Just assign a figure from 0 to 10, where 0 means your president could have no influence on this target or individual and 10 means your president could have full influence with this target or individual.

11.   Then take each point of column 4, and put a "*" (star) on the right side of that column for the points that are the most important for you, for your conference, and for your daily job.

12.   This is an important part, so please do this classification carefully.

13.   Then for each of the points with a "star," in the same fourth column, write down some ideas or ways that your president could increase his/her influence to help you more. There may be several different ways for the same point. You don't have to evaluate the feasibility at this time. Just write down your wishes.

14. At the same time, you can write down how you can get him or her to do that.
15. Write down as it comes to mind all the different ways you think your president could, alone or with your help, increase his or her influence on each target or individual

Spell #5 Magic Word: USE HIM (OR HER)

Mastering Spell #5: How to Make your President Become your Fan

Spell #5: "Make my president happy" is much more powerful than that, as it uses the force of the Internet, search engines, and social media. By now you have started to understand that:
- It is possible to propel individuals on top of search engines that enable them to rank when people make searches for your market main keywords.
- It is possible to set up viral strategies to spread your messages and get new prospects in your industry using social media.

You will be amazed to set up the "Conference President Synergy System." This is an advanced personality program focused on one personality: your president.

As well as for your best speakers, when you master Spell#5 at full strength:
- You will be able to propel your president on the Internet in a way that:
  o does not require more than a few hours of his or her time
  o dramatically enhances his or her reputation on the Internet
  o propels him or her on the Internet search engines

Your president will thank you for the extensive media and Internet coverage that he or she will have on his or her other activities, whatever they are. The beauty is that it is a win-win program because the president system that we will build for your event will propel your president AND, at the same time, link him or her to your conference.

He or she will have, as a result of your "Conference President Synergy System," his or her own active social media strategy, producing results for all of his or her other activities as well.

That strategy will be aligned with your conference so that all the benefits will be both for you and for your president. As a consequence of the success of this synergy between your president and your conference, he or she will have a hands-on involvement in all other aspects of the event.

Chapter 8

Spell #6: Make my Next Conference the Most Successful and Memorable one for my Participants

Making our next conference the most memorable and successful one is the ultimate goal for each of us as conference people. To reach that objective, the easiest way is to step into the shoes of our customers.

What would make our event memorable for them?

We will start by asking ourselves the question for attendees. The same exercise can be done for exhibitors and sponsors.

So what do participants want from your conference?

How do you add value to your conference from a professional point of view?

What is the best way to make your participants come back?

Whether we like it or not, we are in an area where everything comes down to the bottom line. Therefore the best way to attract customers to your conference and to make them come back is to arrange things so that they sign the maximum number of deals.

From your side, that means being able to provide them with the most efficient ways to identify their best matching persons and to be able to have them connect efficiently.

You cannot neglect to offer them this highly valuable service. It is important that you choose the technology that is appropriate to your target audience.

Any system that will maximize the deals among participants is a must for any conference person who wants to secure the loyalty of his or her customers.

Building a strong network for career propelling or career protection is a major, often non-expressed, motivation. Therefore the services you offer them to optimize their contacts has a double benefit.

The Five Extra "Somethings" to Your Keynotes and Sessions

The second part of your participants' motivation is to get the ultimate information about your industry:
- from your speakers, keynotes, and sessions
- from browsing through the exhibition area
-

They need to:
- have access to the information
- gather the information of interest to them
- bring it back home
- if appropriate, report the information to their team and to their boss
- in certain circumstances, convince their boss or their team to implement a new strategy they bring back

Your role is to help them by making these five particular approaches to getting and using information as efficient as possible.

How to Help your Participants Efficiently Access Information

In the era of iPhones, iPads, 3D TV, and holographic virtual conferencing, do you think that your participants are still willing to find which session to attend or which booth to visit in a hundred-page, four-pound directory?

The time to provide them with electronic, easily accessible maps and schedules that are integrated into their mobile devices and schedule applications has come.

Even if you choose to keep paper-based directories and schedules to destinations on hand for an older crowd, you cannot avoid initiating the transition and providing both supports, starting now.

How to Help your Participants Easily Gather Information and Bring it Back Home

What is the size of the welcome package that you hand over to your attendees? Perhaps it's better to say "What is the weight of the bag they carry when they leave the conference area?"

Do you think we are still in an era where you bring an additional ten-pound piece of luggage full of the documents back home?

Allowing for an in-between period for older audiences, you must also use digital documents and provide everything they can bring back from your conferences on digital support, whether they are on PDFs, audios, mp3s, or videos.

It is your role to ensure your exhibitors do the same. Providing them the technologies to do this can be part of the additional services offered to them and supplemental revenues for you.

I suggest you apply the same method for yourself. I always wonder why meeting planners continue to carry massive paper binders when on-site.

I'd like to share with you a memorable debate at a conference roundtable, which I remember set the tone for the general mindset:

-..."*a planner's job is to plan for the unpredictable. Sometimes technology fails. My binder that has everything about the meeting from attendees to room lists to transportation and dinner contracts is my lifesaver.*"
- *Sometimes cars fail, so should you take your horse?*
- *[laughs]*
- *It is also quicker to find information in a well-organized binder.*
- *[laughs]*
- *In fact, I use technology but I still carry a folder for security.*
- *[laughs]*
- *Things can break, but the trusty binder keeps everything you need in one place.*
- *[laughs]*
- *I know it seems archaic, but it really works...*
- *[laughs]*
- *If you have a well-organized binder, it's just faster.*
- *[laughs]*
- *My binder is my bible that I'm never without.*
- *[laughs]*
- *After fifteen-plus years in the event biz, I never leave home without my binder.*
- *[laughs]*

- I keep the binder in the car for "just in case" accidents.

- [laughs]

- I just like my paper.

- [laughs]

- I read much better when it is on paper than on a screen.

- [laughs]

Unfortunately, this conversation is real. This is not a comic sketch.

The pace has definitely picked up. We as conference people must jump on the technology train. Those who don't will stay stranded like those in dying, old, desert cowboy towns.

How to Help your Participants use the Information to Report to and Convince their Team or Boss

We have all attended a conference where we found the ultimate strategy we'd like to implement upon our return. Everything seemed easy and clear when the speaker was describing all the benefits.

However, everything became blurred and more complicated when we reported about it to a team or boss who was not there, did not experience the intensity of the event, or got so wrapped up in their day-to-day work that they were far from being receptive to new, "disruptive" ideas.

It is your role to train your speakers to provide attendees with a digital "give-away." It can be as simple as a link you can access to ready-to-use PowerPoint presentation extracts for when they report back to their companies.

How to Add Value with your Conference from a Personal Point of View

What will your Participants Remember from your Conference?

If you remember the events you attended, you know that the most vivid memories are rarely from professional encounters but from personal ones.

Enabling your participants to enjoy their spare time is key. Time off is often rare during a conference. Therefore it should be well planned out.

It is part of our job as conference organizers to offer our participants a pre-planned list of "what-to-dos" after their working day: where to have dinner, where to stay fit and run, where to relax and listen to music, where to dance or party (if appropriate), where to play golf, how to visit a historical city, how to enjoy the beach facilities, etc.

All these take planning, and we know perfectly well how to do that. It's our job! But beyond that, what will make the difference for a participant is a specific encounter, a person that he or she will meet and share his or her interests with, with whom he or she will possibly enjoy a satisfying dinner, discussing a passion for ancient Asian art or the city they were both brought up in.

Setting up an efficient networking system that will help people meet the right person that will make his or her spare time memorable is now essential for your conference to be outstanding.

Several technologies are designed for that. Among those we have tested, most are at the pre-historic stage.

Some, on the other hand, are advanced and able to assist you in providing this great service to your customers.

How to Make Spouses Fans of your Conference

Travelling to conferences may not be so easy for a family or couple. Yet spouses are often happy to take the opportunity to visit new cities. Conference producers now are starting to prepare lists of extra-curricular activities for participants' spouses.

It is now time to go further and use the same tools and technologies to plan for the well-being of companions as the ones described above to make the event memorable for the attendees.

Re-engineering your Conference to Match new Consumption Patterns

An emerging and relatively new type of information consumption behavior is multi-tasking.

To understand what this concept means, I encourage you to watch your children or the ones around you. They really do several different things at a time. They text their friends while browsing the Internet and/or watching a movie. Unless they have been educated not to behave this way, our children and the younger people among us are more and more apt to indulge in these habits.

Ten years ago we would have stopped what we were doing when receiving a phone call on our landline. But who these days remains motionless while having a conversation on a mobile?

When my daughter was five years old, I was afraid she would have difficulties focusing at school because she was always doing several things at a time. I am now relieved to understand she really is into each of the tasks she manages to perform simultaneously.

We have done a lot of research about social media, including with U.S. and European universities. I remember a story about a recognized professor from Paris-La Sorbonne Sociology University (the French "Berkeley") of his discovery of the new multi-tasking pattern of information consumption.

"...That was in 2005, at the rise of social networks. I was having a lecture about traditional tribes versus electronic tribes. As I was speaking about the Internet, I noticed that most of my students were focused on typing on their laptops. I was telling myself that I was blessed to have such serious students using technology to take the notes from my lecture. I was intrigued and curious about what I observed. And when I got down from the platform, and walked in the aisles, I was hypnotized by what I discovered. It was so new for me! I could see all the screens of these opened laptops. And then I might have had a heart attack.

Most of the laptops had screens split into two parts. One part was a text processor (and I hope it was opened for my course). On the other side, some were browsing the Internet, others were watching movies, others were sending e-mails, and still others were on Facebook.

I actually ran back to my chair on the platform, sat down, and breathed as if I had a dizzy spell. My thoughts were clashing. I was torn between getting rid of all of them, quitting, resigning...I was so upset that I ended the lecture. I remember their expressions full of incomprehension. There was definitely a mutual lack of understanding.

In the days that followed that incident, I called in three of my students in order to discuss with them what was wrong with my course. I was ready for the worst, ready to hear that my lectures were so boring that...

In fact I had the breakthrough of my life. They congratulated me on my teaching. When I asked them to convince me that they were not toadying to me, they brought back such detailed parts of my course lectures that I was obliged to believe they were really multi-tasking.

They even told me that they were looking for supplementary information on the Internet in real time while preparing their case. Some could have been viewing blockbuster trailers, but I realized that they were able to capture a lot of information in regard to the class lecture at the same time. And I dare to say that I envy their productiveness. I wish I could have done the same during my studies..."

I like this story because it describes precisely how more and more of your attendees will want to consume the information from your conference. You have to be part of this trend and provide them the tools to multi-task.

Spell #6 Magic Word: TECHNOLOGY

Mastering Spell #6: Make my Next Conference the Most Successful and Memorable for my Participants

When you master Spell #6 at full strength, the "Conference Memorable Event System" will give you the capabilities to:

o   Propel your conference to the cutting edge
o   Master the power of social media before, during, and after your event
o   Know and master what information from Linke-din, Facebook, and Twitter will bring results to your conference
o   Enhance your participants' experience, trans-forming your event into a memorable one
o   Increase your bottom line and profits
o   Be recognized as a master in outstanding confer-ences
…and more.

એ∼∽

Chapter 9
Spell #7: Give Me the Power to Stay on top and Turn the Stress Away on Demand

Use the Power of Neuro Linguistic Programming to Defeat Pressure

Neuro Linguistic Programming is a science that is powerfully used either for therapeutic or coaching purposes. Its basic principles are so simple that I am always surprised that it is not more commonly used. If I were in the educational sector, I would definitely teach it to children as soon as they were ten or twelve years old and with no hesitation to teenagers forging their identities for the future.

The Personal Goals any Conference Person Should Reach

These tools will help you get through the many stressful situations your conference jobs pose. Your main goals are in regard to:

- You and the pressure of the event, including:
  o being highly capable in managing the multiple tasks that event organizing requires
  o being able to make the optimum decision on the fly
  o managing priorities when necessary
- You and your team, including:
  o performing better with less stress in managing your team
  o maintaining your leadership level whatever the circumstances

- You and yourself, including:
    o   regenerating your energy on demand

You and the Pressure of the Event

How to Divide Aftermath Consequences of Issues by Ten

In any of the stressful situations above, there is still something that we have missed. Very often we are able to tell the story afterwards, but in the present, we can't always control everything and have to react to unexpected situations.

All problems cannot be anticipated, but there is a huge difference between detecting the trouble as soon as it starts and patching up the damage once it occurs. Just imagine yourself able to be aware when something is going in the wrong direction at the exact moment it starts to happen.

Awareness is king. In any event, always be present and turn your sensitivity on like a satellite receiver. Listen to your five senses. They always give you the right information in real time. And act as soon as you perceive the signals. Awareness is the first skill you will learn through your "Conference Personal Coaching Program."

The pain will be one-tenth or one Percent.
The energy to restore will be one-tenth or one Percent.

Just becoming aware of a problem at the very moment it starts will bring significant results to you, whereby there is:
- ninety-nine percent less stress
- ninety-nine percent less damage

You and your Team

Training 12: How to Have People do What you Want Them to

Organizing a conference involves permanently asking different people to do multiple tasks for you and endlessly checking that they are correctly done. We as conference people are so often on the move that we are in our own minds and very rarely in the one of the person we are delegating to.

What makes human relationships complicated is that everyone has a hidden agenda. In fact, everyone has a double agenda:
-       his or her professional one
-       his or her personal one

Starting now, before you ask someone to do a specific task for you, ask yourself the following four questions:
-       Question 1: What are the professional reasons this person has an interest in making it work?
-       Question 2: What are the personal reasons this person has an interest in making it work?
-       Question 3: What are the professional reasons this person has an interest in making it not work?
-       Question 4: What are the personal reasons this person has interest in making it not work?

You will be surprised to find the answers to questions 3 and 4. The simple fact that you ask yourself questions 1 and 2 will often change the way you choose to delegate.

Training 13: How to Delegate Powerfully, Reducing the Stress of Wrong Implementation

There are so many delegated tasks in organizing a conference that we often have to choose between two options:
-       Option 1: controlling everything
-       Option 2: relying upon others

It is an incredible dilemma:
-       Choosing option 1 all the time leads to burnout.
-       Choosing option 2 all the time leads to failure.

Sometimes cross-fertilization among different industries is very powerful. There is actually a sector where people are more stressed than ours. Is it possible? Yes. Traders on the stock exchange work in a more intense, stressed environment.

A professional trader always asks herself or himself:
-       "What is the maximum risk I can take?"
-       "What is the minimum risk I cannot take?"

I used to apply the same strategies while delegating tasks for our conferences:
-       "What is the risk I cannot take if the task I have delegated is not done?"
-       "What is the maximum delay I would tolerate if I were unable to check if a task is done without taking an unacceptable risk?"

The answers to these two questions are the secret to finding a medium position and optimizing the ratio between stress and success. They will tell you each time you delegate a task to somebody:

- When you have to first check if the task has been done
- For a repetitious task, how often you have to check if the task is still being done

With these two schedules in your agenda, you will be calm and serene while delegating.

The "Conference Personal Coaching Program" includes templates and worksheets to use on a day-to-day basis, which will dramatically decrease the level of stress induced by the multiple delegations in your job.

You and Yourself

How to Drain off Bad Thoughts in Real Time

Once a problem appears, your capability to solve it, and even to find the best solution, is directly linked to your clarity of mind. If you allow the bad thoughts to take over your mind at that instant, you will suggest and implement the less efficient solution. If you are able to focus on the positive you want to restore, then you will access the best solution.

Training 14: How to Master what you Focus on, Whatever the Circumstances

Mastering what you focus on, whatever the circumstances is king.

1. Before you start this exercise, be sure you have at least an hour available and turn off everything that could disturb you, such as the phone, e-mail, instant messengers, children, or spouse. It is important to do this training in a single stroke and to

stay focused from the beginning to the end. If you don't have one hour, I suggest you pause in your reading and schedule a one-hour appointment with yourself to do this training, which may be the most important of this book. This training is divided into four parts.

2. Try to have two pens of different colors. One pen and a highlighter is a great option.

3. Take a blank sheet of paper. Title it "Positive On-demand."

4. Divide the sheet of paper into two columns.

5. Draw a horizontal line dividing the sheet in two parts.

6. Title the first column "Negative State."

7. Title the second column "Positive State."

8. Title the upper part "The Scene."

9. Title the lower part "My Thoughts."

10. Part 1: The stressful you

11. Remember the last time you were overstressed and definitely in a negative mindset?

12. Close your eyes and review the scene. The more details you recall, the more powerfully you will be able to master your focus the next time you need it.

13. Try to visualize the smallest details. The ones that are connected to the discomfort. Write them down with all the details you can remember. What were you doing? Who was doing what? The place. The colors. The shapes. The clothes. The actors. The actions. Write everything you remember from the scene in the upper part of the first column.

14. Hear every sound, every word that you said or others said. Write them down. The ambient noise, the resonance, the sonorousness, the tonality of your voice, the intonation of others, the silence, if any.

15. Try to remember the smells, the scents.

16. Try to see yourself as in a mirror. Which posture did you have? Which facial expression? How did you swallow? How did you breathe? What were your gestures?

17. What were you thinking at that exact moment? Write everything you remember about your thoughts in the lower part of the first column.

18. Review your left column and add everything that comes to your mind again. Each detail will be used as a weapon later on in this training.

19. When you are done, you can then take the liberty to take a two-minute break to clear your head and remove the negative vibes. Have a glass of water, wash your hands, and listen to your favorite music. But stay focused. Stay here for the second part of the training. Be sure to come back in the next two minutes and not lose the momentum.

20. **Part 2: The invincible you**

21. Now that you are back with a clear mind, remember the last time you felt invincible, capable of everything, unstoppable, and definitely in a positive mindset.

22. Close your eyes and review the scene. The more details you recall, the more powerfully you will be able to master your focus next time you need it.

23. Try to visualize the smallest details. The ones that are connected to the discomfort. Write them down with all the details you can remember. What were you doing? Who was doing what? The place. The colors. The shapes. The clothes. The actors. The actions. Write everything you remember from the scene in the upper part of the second column.

24. Hear every sound, every word that you said or others said. Write them down. The ambient noise, the resonance, the sonorousness, the tonality of your voice, the intonation of others, the silence, if any.

25. Try to remember the smells, the scents.
26. Try to see yourself as in a mirror. Which posture did you have? Which facial expression? How did you swallow? How did you breathe? What were your gestures?
27. What were you thinking at this exact moment? Write everything you remember about your thoughts in the lower part of the second column.
28. Review the right column and add everything that comes to your mind again. Each detail will be used as a weapon later on in this training.
29. **Part 3: Your triggers to negativity**
30. When you are done, we can now enter the third part of this training: the transformation part.
31. Take your other colored pen or the highlighter.
32. In the upper part of the first column, circle every detail that seems to be common to frequent situations where you feel bad.
33. Do it carefully.
34. In the lower part of the first column, circle every detail that seems to be common to frequent situations where you feel bad.
35. Do it carefully.
36. Review what you have circled in the left column to be sure you didn't forget anything.
37. All that you have circled is silver. They are the triggers that set your mindset into a negative state. They are the way you behave in bad situations. They are the thoughts that usually fill your mind when you enter a stressful state.
38. Study them. Be aware of them. They will be your signals next time that will tell you: Stop. Transform your state from negative to positive.
39. **Part 4: Your triggers to invincibility and positive energy**
40. Take your other colored pen or highlighter.

41. In the upper part of the second column, circle every detail that seems to be common to frequent situations when you feel unstoppable with overflowing positive energy.
42. Do it carefully.
43. In the lower part of the second column, circle every detail that seems to be common to frequent situations where you feel invincible and in a very positive mindset.
44. Do it carefully.
45. Review what you have circled in the right column to be sure you didn't forget anything.
46. All that you have circled is gold. They are the instant buttons that you will use to set your mindset in the positive state on demand. They are indicative of the way you behave in great situations. They are the thoughts that usually fill your mind when you enter a positively determined state.
47. Study them. Be aware of them. They will be your weapons next time that will tell you: Go! Transform your state from negative to positive.

You deserve a pause. You deserve some time to assimilate this fundamental training. Once you integrate it, you will start having the power to get rid of your stress on demand. Advanced coaching included in the "Conference Personal Coaching Program" allows you also to switch on your energy on demand. And energy is king for us as conference people.

I will always remember one of our customers saying that she considered herself a great conference person when she finished her day and wasn't tired even when it was late in the night and even when she knew she had done the best job ever...

Training 15: How do I Feel in my Job?

1. Take a blank sheet of paper. Title it "I."
2. Divide the sheet of paper in four columns.
3. Title the first column "+."
4. Title the second column "L" (sad smiley).
5. Title the third column "J" (happy smiley).
6. Title the fourth column "+."
7. Take five to ten minutes to fill in columns 2 and 3.
8. In column 2, write down as they occur to you all the frustrations you have regarding your job, in the short-term as well as the long-term, from small ones to big ones.
9. In column 3, write down as they occur to you all the joys you have regarding your job, in the short-term as well as the long-term, from small ones to big ones.
10. Take a minute or two to verify you haven't forgotten important facts.
11. Then take each point of column 2, and in the first column, just on the left side, put a "*" (star) for the points that are the most important to you.
12. This is an important part, so please do this classification carefully.
13. Then for each of the points with a "star," in the same first column, write down some ideas or ways that you can mitigate or decrease this frustration. There may be several different ways for the same point. You don't have to evaluate the feasibility at this time. Just write down your wishes.
14. Then take each point of column 3, and in the fourth column, just on the right side, put a "*" (star) for the points that are the most important to you.
15. This is an important part, so please do this classification carefully.

16. Then for each of the points with a "star," in the same fourth column, write down some ideas or ways that you can improve and increase that point. There may be several different ways for the same point. You don't have to evaluate the feasibility at this time. Just write down your wishes.

This should be an interesting list of possibilities for you to make your daily job easier.

Training 16: The Future of my Career

1. Take a blank sheet of paper. Title it "The future of my career."
2. Divide the sheet of paper in five columns.
3. Title the first column "Now."
4. Title the second column "Next Year."
5. Title the third column "in 3 Years."
6. Title the fourth column "in 10 Years."
7. Title the fifth column "+."
8. Draw a horizontal line in the middle of your page.
9. Draw a big "+" in the upper side of the page.
10. Draw a big "−" in the upper side of the page.
11. Take five to ten minutes to fill in column 1.
12. Where are you now?
13. What is great about where you are? Answers go in the upper part of the first column (big + part).
14. What is bad about where you are? What disturbs you? Answers go in the lower part of the first column (big—part).
15. In column 2, where will you be next year if nothing changes?
16. For each of the good things, will they still be there? If yes, write them down again in the upper part of the second column.

17. For each of the bad things, will they still be there? If yes, write them down again in the lower part of the second column.
18. In column 3, where will you be three years from now if nothing changes?
19. For each of the good things, will they still be there? If yes, write them down again in the upper part of the second column.
20. For each of the bad things, will they still be there? If yes, write them down again in the lower part of the second column.
21. In column 4, where you will be ten years from now if nothing changes?
22. For each of the good things, will they still be there? If yes, write them down again in the upper part of the second column.
23. For each of the bad things, will they still be there? If yes, write them down again in the lower part of the second column.
24. In the upper part of column 5, for each of the good things, write down what you have to do to be sure they will still be there ten years from now.
25. In the lower part of column 5, for each of the bad things, write down what you have to do to prevent them from being there ten years from now.

This should be an interesting list of possibilities for you to make your future job better.

Training 17: Your Commitments

1. Take a blank sheet of paper. Title it "My Action Plan."
2. Divide the sheet of paper in three columns.
3. Title the first column "Action."
4. Title the second column "By."
5. Title the third column "Resources."

6. Go back to the sheet of paper called "The future of my career."
7. Copy out the actions you wrote down in the last column of the "The future of my career" worksheet.
8. In the second column, commit yourself to doing this action BY X date. Could be tomorrow, could be in one month, in three months, in one year from now, but it has to be a commitment from you. Certainly the sooner, the better. Be realistic. Be daring.
9. In the third column, write down the resources that can help you reach this goal. These can include money, people, mentors, leaning, training...
10. This is an important part, so please take all the time necessary to do this brainstorming carefully.

This should be an interesting list of possibilities for you to make your future job better.

Training 18: Action

1. Take a blank sheet of paper. Title it "It's My Time."
2. Draw a horizontal line in the middle of the page.
3. The title in the upper part of the page should be "My Decisions Today."
4. Take five to ten minutes to write down in the upper part of the page the two decisions that you know you have to make but have been postponing for a while. What are the decisions you have to make today and that will change your life in the direction you want it to go?
5. The title of the upper part of the page is "My Actions Today."
6. Take five to ten minutes to write down in the lower part of the page the two immediate actions you

will take or decisions you will make immediately to shape the future of your conference career as you want it to be.

This should be an interesting list of possibilities to make your future job better. Just do it now!

Spell #7 Magic Word: YOUR FUTURE IS WHAT MATTERS

Mastering Spell #7: How to Manage your Energy and Stress on Demand

When you master Spell #7 at full strength, the "Successful Conference Personal Coaching Program" will give you the capabilities to:

- o   Deal with a big team
- o   Deal with difficult persons
- o   Manage your time for organizing an event effectively with a huge list of "must-do" tasks
- o   Delegate effectively, through a control process, to part-time, one-time-only staff
- o   Manage priorities
- o   Make difficult decisions, using a decision-making process that lowers the downsides of a bad decision and emphasizes the upsides of a good decision
- o   Connect to your energy reservoir on demand, even after being on-site for several days and experiencing nights of non-stop event management
- o   Manage your stress by deleting bad emotions as soon as they come up and killing them while they are still at a manageable level

...and much more.

Chapter 10
The Successful Conference Academy

The Successful Conference Academy has been founded in order to:

- Help conference people and trade show people adapt themselves to the profound changes in our industry
- Enable them to master the new rules and strategies
- Help them understand the technologies that matter for their events and to identify which of them can effectively bring results to their particular market, audience, and conference.

Successful Conference has developed "done-for-you" Conference Systems that are customized for your event, implemented for you and with you, bringing you results in the seven major areas of our conference job, meaning:

- Producing
- Marketing
- Promoting
- Selling
- Organizing
- Supervising the event
- Managing the team

୬ଏ

Chapter 11
The New "Conference People 2.0"

You are Now Part of the "Conference People 2.0"

Where Does this Name Come From?

What a funny name!

Remember when the Internet was invented? Great invention!
Remember the Internet bubble?
2000, 2001. Lots of deaths among the Internet players.

But the Internet people survived. They re-invented themselves.

In 2005 the rules changed. The power of the Internet changed hands—from the technical guys creating websites to the users. That was a great revolution. They created a new Internet more powerful, stronger, more capable of withstanding upcoming crises, and they renamed it "Internet 2.0."

I love this phrase from H.G. Wells:

"Adapt or perish, now as ever, is nature's inexorable imperative."

That's exactly what "Conference People 2.0" is all about: conference people who have new skills, are more powerful, stronger, and more capable of withstanding upcoming crises and adapting to changes.

And this is so important because our conference industry has been facing big challenges for several years. Old-minded conference persons even say that the conference industry is in a deep crisis.

"Conference People 2.0" are above the crowd, are at the cutting edge of our industry, and are therefore protected from downsides.

The conference industry has changed and is continuing to change. Because to change is difficult and not to change is fatal, "Conference people 2.0" change themselves before they become obsolete.

We invented that name "Conference People 2.0" just for fun. Yet it clearly differentiates those who stay in the crisis from those who use opportunities like the Internet and social media (and others) to get to the top of our conference industry. And now you know what the difference means.

Ask yourself this question: Who are the three persons that you admire the most?
1.
2.
3.

What has he or she done to make you admire him or her?
1.
2.
3.
Why do you admire him or her for having done the above?
1.
2.
3.

There is a high probability that your answers to these questions will indicate that you admire certain persons because they hold attitudes that have empowered them to impress you and others. Everything is a question of attitude.

If you remember only ONE thing from this book or video, I hope it will be that your future, your success one year from now, three years from now, ten years from now depends on your attitude now.

Do you want to stay on the down-slope of the declining conference industry? Or do you want to bring your next conference, your career, and your life to the next level and become one of the unstoppable "Conference People 2.0?"

I like your answer.
The Future Will Belong To The Unafraid.
Welcome to the "Conference People 2.0"

Your best wishes for your next conference

Is there a spell or a wish you'd really want for your day-to-day conference job?

What are your best wishes for your next successful conference?

Just ask here:

http://www.successfulconference.com/best-wishes-for-your-successful- conference

More Free Conference Training

You can get frequent updates and additional free training on:

Successful Conference Official Website:
      http://www.successfulconference.com
Successful Conference Blog:
      http://www.successfulconference.com/blog

Join us on Facebook for daily tips and upgrades:
      http://www.facebook.com/successfulconference

Join us on Twitter for news in real time:
      http://www.twitter.com/successfulconf

Transforming your conference organization

If you are responsible for a multi-conference organization with multiple parallel events and an important team, you may find tremendous assistance to transform your whole organization:

-   With the INSTRUCTOR GUIDE linked to this book, describing how to teach and transmit the key principles contained in "the7 Spells of the new Conference People 2.0".

-   With the Conference Organization Transformation Coaching services provided by the Successful Conference team.

http://www.successfulconference.com/tranforming-your-conference-organization

Participating to our International Survey about Confer-ence Excellence

You can participate to this "must be known" interna-tional survey at

> http://www.succesfulconference.com/
> international-conference-survey

and you will:

- share the best practices, and cross-fertilize with conference people from other countries.
- get the results for free before they are published.

Appendix 1
For Convention Centers

If you are working for a convention center, your customers are the conferences and trade shows that you host. Certainly you should focus on satisfying their requirements as they are paying your salary.

In this book, you will discover what makes the difference between a traditional convention center having a hard time staying in the competition and maintaining revenues and signing with new events and convention centers that are at the culling edge of our industry, venues where every event planner wants their event to take place.

There is a dedicated website with plenty of training just for you, produced by the Successful Conference convention center experts' team at:
http://www.conventioncentertochoose.com

A "Convention center to choose" changes itself before it becomes obsolete. It is all about understanding exactly what being a "convention center to choose" means and how you can attract more new events and increase your profits.

We invented the name "convention center to choose" because it appropriately describes what differentiates those who will stay in the crisis from those who will use opportunities like the Internet and social media (and others) to be at the top of our convention industry. And you will see the difference before the end of this book.

"Convention center to choose" is an invitation-only membership website designed by conference people for conference people, where every month you will find the latest winning strategy used by the top-gun convention centers all around the world. We will bring to you only goal-oriented strategies with a track record of amazing results. Everything is about attracting more new events and increasing your revenues and profits.

Experts from all over the world from our convention industry will appear on what we call our TV channel. And every episode comes with a bonus, which is a marketing tool that you can immediately use for your prospects and the events that you'd like to sign up with.

These strategies are all bottom line-oriented, and provided is a precise and easy-to-follow guideline for how to dominate your industry with your convention center using the new tools that count for your market.

Free preview at: http://www.conventioncentertochoose.com

Appendix 2
For Venues

If you are working for a venue as a conference person, your customers are the conferences and events that you host. Certainly you should focus on satisfying their requirements as they are paying your salary.

In this book, you will discover what makes the difference between old-guard venues that are having a hard time staying in the competition, experiencing difficulties maintaining their revenues, and signing with new events and venues that are at the cutting edge of our industry.

There is a dedicated website with frequent training just for you, produced by the Successful Conference venues experts' team at:
http://www.venuetochoose.com

A "Venue to choose" changes itself before it becomes obsolete. It is all about understanding exactly what being a "venue to choose" means and how you can attract more new events and increase your profits.

We invented the name "venue to choose" because it provides a meaningful image that differentiates those who will stay in the crisis from those who will use all these opportunities like the Internet and social media (and others) to get to the top of our convention industry. And you will see the difference before the end of this book.

"Venue to choose" is an invitation-only membership website designed by conference people for conference people, where every month you will find the latest winning strategy used by the top-gun venues and convention centers all around the world. We will bring to you only goal-oriented strategies with a track record of amazing results. Everything is about attracting more new events and increasing your revenues and profits.

Convention industry experts from all over the world will appear on what we call our TV channel. And every episode comes with a bonus, which is a marketing tool that you can immediately use for identifying your prospects and the events that you'd like to sign up with.

The strategies are bottom line-oriented and are precisely mapped out. Included are easy-to-follow guidelines for how to dominate your industry with your venue, using new tools that count for your market.

Free preview at:
http://www.venuetochoose.com

Appendix 3
Testimonials

Jonathan, medical conference multi-producer:

"...One thousand thanks to this book, which is as easy to read as it is powerful when the strategies it contains are applied. I blew away all my team with my last conference..."

Mariella, auto trade show executive:

"...This book has been like a wake-up from a nightmare. I became aware of what was going wrong in the conference world and with me, and it gave me the direction to climb up over the clouds and find a new positive path for my career..."

Edouard, convention center CEO:

"...What our customers as event organizers want has changed. This new awareness is a breakthrough I discovered page after page in this book. I was able to transform my team's mindset from discouraged to highly motivated. I ask all my team members to read this book as a common guideline for each of us..."

A joint publication in
The Successful Conference Series
www.successfulconference.com

CPSIA information can be obtained at www.ICGtesting.com
Printed in the USA
LVOW07s2011201015

459026LV00031B/993/P